BEES

PowerKiDS press™

New York

Suzanne Slade

To my mother, Martha, the "Queen" bee of the Buckingham family

Published in 2008 by The Rosen Publishing Group, Inc.
29 East 21st Street, New York, NY 10010

First Edition

Editor: Joanne Randolph
Book Design: Julio Gil
Photo Researcher: Nicole Pristash

Photo Credits: Cover, pp. 1, 5, 7, 9, 11, 13, 15, 17, 19, 21 © Shutterstock.com; pp. 7 (inset), 11 (inset) © Dennis Kunkel Microscopy, Inc.

Library of Congress Cataloging-in-Publication Data

Slade, Suzanne.
  Bees / Suzanne Slade. — 1st ed.
    p. cm. — (Under the microscope: Backyard bugs)
  ISBN-13: 978-1-4042-3822-0 (library binding)
  ISBN-10: 1-4042-3822-0 (library binding)
  1. Bees—Juvenile literature. I. Title.
  QL565.2.S53 2008
  595.79'9—dc22
                                    2007005790

Manufactured in the United States of America

Contents

What's Buzzing in Your Backyard?

   Your backyard is filled with colorful flowers, plants, and trees. Lots of different animals live there, too. Squirrels, birds, and many types of **insects** make their home in your backyard habitat. A habitat is a place where certain plants and animals naturally live.

   When you sit in your backyard on a hot summer day, listen carefully. You may hear a tiny sound. Buzz! That sound is a bee. When bees shiver their wings, they make a buzzing noise. Bees like to visit the flowers in your backyard.

This bee is about to land on a flower and drink its nectar, the sweet juice in it. Bees visit hundreds of flowers in a day.

Bee Business

Bees are busy workers. They have important business in your backyard. Bees must land on flowers so they can drink nectar.

As a bee drinks nectar, a fine yellow dust found inside a flower sticks to the bee's legs. This dust is called pollen. A bee may carry 50,000 pieces of pollen at one time. As bees visit other flowers, they spread this pollen around. Pollen helps plants make new seeds. Trees need pollen to make fruit, such as apples. Bees also give pollen to their young to eat.

This bee has gathered a lot of pollen in the pollen baskets on its legs. *Inset:* This is a close-up look at the pollen basket.

Magnification: x 8

Types of Bees

Would you believe there are about 20,000 different kinds of bees? One of the most commonly known is the honeybee. Honeybees are very social. They like to live with other bees in a **colony**. A honeybee colony may have up to 50,000 bees. Another common and social bee is the bumblebee. This yellow and black bee has a fat, furry body.

Not all bees live in colonies. A leaf-cutting bee lives alone. It lays its eggs on curled leaves. Another bee that lives by itself is called the carpenter bee. Carpenter bees live in pieces of dead wood.

This large, fuzzy bee is a bumblebee. Most bumblebees are gentle, or not likely to hurt anyone.

Discover the Bee

Like all insects, a bee's body has three parts. It is made of a head, thorax, and abdomen. A bee has five eyes on its head. The two large **compound eyes** see movement. Its three smaller eyes, called simple eyes, see the amount of light ahead. At the top of a bee's head are two **antennae**. Antennae help bees smell.

The thorax is the middle part of a bee. Four wings and six legs are found on the thorax.

The long, thin tail on a bee is called the abdomen. Some bees have a sharp **stinger** on their abdomen.

This is a labeled photo of a bee's head. *Inset:* Many bees have a stinger on their abdomen. Bees use their stinger to keep their hives safe.

Simple Eyes

Antennae

Compound Eyes

Mouth

Magnification: x 22

11

Honeybee Life Cycle

Bees begin life as an egg and then go through three more life stages. The amount of time spent at each stage is different for different kinds of bees.

A tiny honeybee egg will **hatch** in three days. The newly hatched honeybee larva is white and shaped like a piece of rice. As its body becomes larger, the honeybee larva will **shed** its outer skin. After shedding four times, a larva spins a **cocoon** around itself. Inside the cocoon, the larva turns into a pupa. The pupa changes into an adult honeybee 12 days later.

This photo shows how a bee looks as it moves through its life cycle from larva (top left) to adult bee (bottom right).

Baby Bees

The queen bee is the most important bee in a colony. She is the only bee that can lay eggs. The male, or boy, bees are called drones. Their only job is to **mate** with the queen. Upon finishing this job, drones leave the colony and die.

After mating, a queen flies to her hive and begins laying eggs. She places one egg in each hive cell. Once the eggs hatch, worker bees feed the larvae a mix of pollen and honey. Worker bees build the hive, clean, hunt, and feed the young.

Here worker bees care for larvae in the honeycomb cells. Worker bees are female bees that cannot lay eggs.

Dinner Dance

Worker bees must find flowers when they get hungry. They eat pollen and use nectar to make honey. A bee colony works together to find food. One bee can tell others where to find flowers by doing a dance, called a waggle dance. A bee walks in the shape of the number eight when doing this dance. It shows in which direction and how far away the flowers are.

It was long thought that bees did a second dance when flowers were close to the hive. This was called the round dance. Now people think this is just a shorter waggle dance.

A worker bee sucks nectar from flowers with a long pipe on its head, called a glossa, which can be seen here.

Be Careful, Bee!

Bees face many dangers in the world. In some countries, there are very few honeybees left. New buildings and roads force bee colonies out of their habitats. Bees are killed by pests. Some have traveled from other parts of the world. The wax moth from Russia lays its eggs in beehives. When these eggs hatch, wax-moth larvae eat honey and **beeswax** inside the hive.

Another bug, the varroa mite, lives on honeybees and sucks their blood. This mite also eats honeybee eggs and larvae. Mites can kill a whole colony of bees.

Large spiders are an enemy of the bee. This spider has caught and killed a bee, which it will soon eat.

Hooray for Honey

When the weather gets cold, honeybees must stay in their hives to keep warm. They eat honey they have stored in hive cells during the winter. These cells have six sides and are made of beeswax. Honeybees use nectar to make honey.

A colony makes three times as much honey as the bees in it will eat. **Beekeepers** gather extra honey from hives. This extra honey is used by people. It is hard to get honey out of natural hives, so most beekeepers build a hive called an apiary. An apiary is made of wood and has trays that slide out. Bees put their honey in these wooden trays.

For over 4,000 years, people have been keeping bees and gathering extra honey for people to eat. This beekeeper removes a tray that bees have filled with honey.

Busy Bees

Bees have lived on Earth for millions of years. People know this because some early bees were trapped in resin, a sticky juice from trees, and were later discovered. The first bees helped people and plants, just like bees do today. Bees **pollinate** more than 90 different crops, including oranges, raspberries, almonds, and apples.

Do you love the sweet taste of honey? Most people eat about 1 pound (.5 kg) each year. Worker bees fly about 55,000 miles (88,514 km) and get nectar from two million flowers to make 1 pound (.5 kg) of honey. Bees are very busy helping people!

Glossary

antennae (an-TEH-nee) Thin, rodlike feelers on the head of certain animals.

beekeepers (BEE-kee-perz) People who raise bees.

beeswax (BEEZ-wax) Wax that is made by bees.

cocoon (KUH-koon) A soft outer covering that some bugs put around themselves as they grow.

colony (KAH-luh-nee) A large group of insects that live and work together.

compound eyes (KOM-pownd EYZ) The larger eyes of bugs, which are made up of many simple eyes.

hatch (HACH) To come out of an egg.

insects (IN-sekts) Small animals that often have six legs and wings.

mate (MAYT) To come together to make babies.

pollinate (PAH-luh-nayt) To move pollen around to different plants, which helps them make seeds.

shed (SHED) To get rid of an outside covering, like skin.

stinger (STING-er) A sharp point on the back end of an insect that it can use to hurt enemies.

Index

Web Sites

Due to the changing nature of Internet links, PowerKids Press has developed an online list of Web sites related to the subject of this book. This site is updated regularly. Please use this link to access the list:
www.powerkidslinks.com/umbb/bee/

24